First book published by

Nthebe Works

PASSION

EXPRESSED

Contains Four Chapters…

1. Knowing life
2. Knowing love
3. Letting go
4. Starting afresh

For everyone to enjoy…

Contents

Knowing Life 1

Knowing Love 39

Letting Go 75

    Step 1: It is not your fault 82

    Step 2: It's his loss 87

    Step 4: Be determined to let go 95

    Step 5: Get rid of what's his 103

    Step 6: Let the pain out 112

    Step 7: Ask for social support 115

    Step 8: Forgive 118

Starting Afresh 126

References 152

Copyright © 2018

Original literary work by: Tselane Grace Nthebe

Edited by: Tselane Grace Nthebe

Copyedited by: Meagan Zealand

Front cover by: Nthebe Works

nthebeworks@gmail.com

064 075 1603

086 606 5029

Printed by: Red Spiral

1219 Rooi-els Street Moregloed Pretoria 0186

Info@redspiral.co.za

012 333 4513

ISBN 978-0-620-64048-0

First published in book form in Bloemfontein,

November 2018

The author's rights have been affirmed.

No unauthorized copying

Any copying, uploading, scanning and any form of electronic sharing of any part of this book without the author's permission is piracy and theft of intellectual property of the author.

Obtain permission to use author's material at

nthebeworks@gmail.com

Foreword

In my first few years as a University student I learned a number of things. Firstly, I learned that 24 hours are not enough to provide a chance of being a successful student and having a life. Secondly, I learned that sleep was something I was not ready to miss as much as I did and thirdly, I learned I was not as much of a grown up as I had insisted I was to my parents. In these early years I was lucky enough to meet the author of the book you are about to read. We became fast friends and she unknowingly taught me that the lessons I had learned truly were unfounded. Here was a bright and independent woman, working her way towards greatness and the rest of us could only wish that we could work as hard. Very quickly my sleepless nights and declaration of not having time proved to be excuses in the light of someone who so easily mastered these things. The fact that I wasn't as grown up as I thought just turned out to be the truth, surprise, surprise.

Fast-forward a few years and she has become a mother, a graduate, a student, a published poet, now a published author and a mogul. She has become a woman we can all learn from and, lucky for us, she has given us these lessons in a wonderful book full of witty comments that will have you laughing out loud and admitting to yourself that you may just be hiding away from the glaring truth of how you may be holding yourself back after all.

By now, you must be desperate to move on from the longwinded foreword that you accidentally thought was a part of the book (what a champ you are for getting this far), and I will let you go with the following warning.

This book may cause you to kick yourself into gear, and it may teach you to be honest with yourself about the way you go about your life. It's a kick in the pants, it's up to you to decide if you're willing to take the chance and read it.

Greetings from an undeserving nobody

Meagan Zealand

Knowing Life

Life can become very difficult. People often wonder why I even have the audacity to say that because I am not even 25. However, to me life is difficult nonetheless.

Growing up, I always associated myself with people older than me, which I believe contributed a lot to my current approach towards life. During this process I got to know life, or at least the fundamentals of it. I then ended up formulating what I call *The basic recipe of growth* containing three easy steps that are guaranteed to lead to one's growth.

Step 1: You must acknowledge your mistakes. You must become aware of what you have done… How else will you know that what you have done is wrong if you do not acknowledge it at all?

Step 2: You need to accept that you have made a mistake. You have to accept that you have wasted time and that you acted out of foolishness. You have to admit that you messed things up really badly. You have to acknowledge that you acted like a person with no purpose in life. It is only once you start accepting this that your growth will start taking place.

Step 3: You have to build up. You have to commit yourself to changing your situation. Overall, change is not something that can occur spontaneously, you have to build it from the ground up.

Life needs commitment and once you feel that things are too hard for you; that is when you need to intensify your praying. That is when you need to go on your knees and talk to God.

In one of his sermons, Pastor Att Boshoff once mentioned that when one becomes more successful, a lot of pressure will often build up. And that is when one's faith becomes tested and your actual character is revealed. It is therefore only once you learn to acknowledge and accept what you have done, that you will be able to fix your mistakes. Remember not to do things just for the sake of doing them because "by-the-way things will give you by-the-way results".

I love growth because it is one of the greatest challenges that one has to go through in order to be able to start the journey of life. From birth till grade 12 you are alive but you only start living after matric. It therefore becomes extremely important for you to start thinking about the seeds that you want to plant while you are still alive in order to reap the fruit you want once you start living.

What is important for you to know is that everything is up to you. The way you handle situations in your life is up to you. You and only you can set and direct your compass to reach the destination that you want to reach. However, the advice I want to give to you, is that you should know what you want! Set your goals and work hard to meet those particular goals. Success will not just fall in your lap, you have to build it and it is not easy.

Take it like your mother when you were just two gametes fused together as a zygote attached to her uterus lining. Think about the excitement your mother felt knowing that after nine months you would be in her arms. Think of all the changes she had to go through just so you could survive…The bad habits she had to quit…The mood swings…cravings…weight gain…eating healthy.

Not everyone can go through that but she did. She was happy each time she threw up because she knew that with each day that passes, she was closer to having you in her arms. Finally, you were born... You are your mother's success. Approach life like that...Accept challenges, conquer them even if you do not win, the thing that counts is that at least you tried.

It is vital for you to know that you are your mother's success. Hence, you should feel like a success, act like a success, walk like a success and dream of excelling and making your life a success. You were not brought to earth just so you can die. It is even stated in the Bible that God has a purpose for your life. It is, however, up to you to search for that purpose and to fulfil it.

You are a blessing to other people's lives. Your life gives someone hope and faith, it is just that you do not know it yet. It is about time you look at yourself in the mirror and see the success, potential, gifts and blessings that are reflecting through your mirror.

Get up! Stand up! Work hard! Live your life to the fullest! Dream big and make your dreams a reality! Leave a legacy, so that when there is no more life in your body, people may remember you as a success. I never said it was easy. I said, get up! The most important thing about doing something is starting with it. This is because in order for you to get somewhere, you need to start somewhere.

I am sure that you have vision; that is why you have to sit down and think about your life…

Make changes where you should and get rid of your bad habits because they are in the way of your prosperity. Do things right so you do not dwell in regrets and "If only I had listened".

You are destined for great things. Go to the "destination" that has your "destiny" so you can prove it to yourself and to others that you are indeed "destined" for greatness, happiness and success through your actions.

You need to be all you can be because a dreamer never dies.

At times, people are afraid of dreaming because they feel their dreams are in vain or simply impossible. Other people are afraid of sharing their dreams because they believe people will laugh at them. Believe me when I tell you that a dreamer never dies. When God is in your dreams, nothing will limit you.

However, you need to be careful who you share your dreams with. Learn to not share your dreams with small minded people. When you want to turn your dreams into reality, you need to stay away from negative people who may want to corrupt your dreams. If you share your dreams with negative and jealous people, they will try to kill your dreams because of the nightmares they are facing in their own lives.

People will always try to discourage you but all you have to do, is keep your head up and focus on your dreams. Remember this all the time: "You must never quit at something simply because someone says you are not good enough".

You have the right to dream and God has given you the right to dream big dreams. However, the only person who can limit your dreams is you. Therefore, I tell you today, "Do not conform to being normal because there is nothing special or unique about being normal".

Keep dreaming and never lose your sense and hunger for expectations. Even if things are not going your way today, keep praying for God is always in control even when things in your life may seem out of control.

Life is very interesting because we all have vision. When I talk about vision, I do not mean fancy cars or mansions…When I talk about vision, I am referring to the means to get those fancy cars or mansions…Your goals…Your career.

A lot of people often say that they want to have certain things by 2020. The real question here is, "What are you doing right now to ensure that you accumulate those things by 2020"?

Vision on its own is useless. In order for our vision to come to life; goals need to be set, hard work needs to be put in and discipline has to be applied. Most of the time, people feel they cannot actualise their dreams because their lives are too cluttered and sometimes in tatters. In other words, these people are afraid they cannot achieve the change that will enable them to exhaust their potential. You need to know that change is possible. Change is attainable. Change is not impossible. Make it a point to prove to yourself that tomorrow you can be a much better person than you are today.

However, the only way you can and will succeed in life is by changing those negatives in your life to positives and also altering those positives in such a way that they lead to your growth.

As humans, we have been created in such a way that, in order for us to survive, we have to go through certain changes and stages. When you are a child you behave like a child. When you are a teen you behave like a teen. And finally, when you are an adult you are ought to behave like an adult. However, you will find it that some people refuse to grow up; in other words they want to remain stagnant. Here is the thing, being stagnant does not necessarily mean that it should literally show that you are standing in one place. Stagnancy could refer to lacking development in your personal life, finances, family, occupation, relationship(s) and education for example. Being stagnant in life can also be seen as a sign of weakness. This is because when you are stuck at one thing the whole time, you cannot measure the change, growth and success in your life.

Change can occur at any time, but consistency is important because it is the key that measures change. It is quite unfortunate that we often relapse and go back to our old ways the second we realize that we actually set goals that are too high for our abilities. A person can decide to stop wearing *Edgars* clothes and start wearing *Louis Vuitton* clothes.

However, a few months down the line, he is back to *Edgars* clothes because he was unable to maintain that status that he created by himself. Here is the thing; no one forces you to do something.

You do it strictly voluntarily. Even if a person persuades or convinces you to do something, you are the one that makes the final decision. What I am saying is simple: "Do not start change that you will not be able to sustain".

One of the reasons why most people lose their motivation and drive in life is because they set goals that are way above their abilities. These people then break down once they fail at what they were trying to achieve. The truth is that life is about growth and experiences.

Life is not like hop scotch where you can skip a few blocks and win the game. It takes baby steps and change in order to make it.

You can achieve positive change, growth and prosperity in your life only if you want to. Luckily, you do not always necessarily need to start your life on a clean slate.

Sometimes you just need to eliminate something so you can prosper, at other times, not.

The only way you can live is by growing and growth is measured by change. However, you can only change by learning and the key to learning is through exposure. Consequently, exposure is gained through seizing opportunities that can add value to your life.

Refuse to conform. Refuse to adapt to stagnancy. Ultimately, the only way you can achieve the state of equilibrium in your life is through constantly and continuously developing yourself.

Do you, make yourself happy because you are you and no one can ever be you. Believe in yourself because if you do not believe in yourself then no one else will.

You also need to have the ability to choose that which is best for your life. You need to have choice in your life. When you do not have the ability to choose, you are bound to fail. When you lack choice automatically you will lack stability. People who lack choice fall for anything because they are unable to stand for something.

Live your life and do what you feel is right for you and your life. Never take anyone's opinion regarding your life into account. If you achieve existence externally you are doomed to self-injury.

In the end, society will always have something to say about you and how you handle things in your life, be it good or bad.

Once you have choice and self-belief, you will never be exposed to stress, depression and self-esteem issues because you will be content with yourself and who you are. Make it a point to develop your own self-identity and most importantly, you should always count your blessings.

As people we often tend to dream a lot and there is absolutely nothing wrong with that. After all, dreams form part of the factors that help us establish who we are and the things that have meaning to us in life. But I am going to tell you this today; "You cannot have everything and keep everything".

What I have realised is that, we always want to add more and more to our material possessions. Yes, it is true that having more possessions makes you seem wealthier but possessions will not make you any happier. Obviously, when you start earning a few rands you become excited.

However, the minute you start earning thousands it becomes more like a "norm" that you have to make money. As a result, it no longer becomes as exciting as it was before. Let me make this clear - You cannot have the best things in life, while keeping the things that you assume are the best things in your life.

Let us take a glass of water to illustrate my point... Imagine you are really, really thirsty and you are yearning for a glass of water. The next thing you are going to do is go to your cupboard to get a glass. Thereafter, you are going to go to the tap to fill it with water. At some point, you are going to have to close your tap because your glass can only contain a certain amount of water. It is common sense that in order for you to have another glass of water, you have to either drink up or throw out the water that is in your glass at that moment.

In reality, the "glass" is your life, the "thirst" represents the dreams and desires you have for your life. The "water" represents the blessings and fruitful rewards that are attainable. Now, as a person you need to quench the "thirst" you have by filling your "glass" with all the best things you can fill it with. However, your "glass" cannot contain all the things you want, hence you will have to let go of the things that you do not really need.

In life, we all have that burning desire to become successful. However, we cannot attain success because we are carrying things that already occupy and strain most of the tools we need to become successful. These things could be friends that always demotivate you, a relationship that is taking most of your time or even substance abuse. Yes, you need friends and a partner in life, but if they are in the way of your goals and future, you will have to let them go. Believe me when I say that you do not need such distractions in your life. The last thing you would want is to wake up one day, after a few years, looking back, thinking of all the things you could have accomplished, had you let go of certain habits or people.

Be in control of your life. Stop allowing people to walk all over you, leaving you to pick up the pieces on your own. Get rid of people that are in the way of your prosperity and growth. Most of the time you will even realise that you do not really need those people.

However, they are still in your life because you are afraid of being alone and of how your life will be without them.

You are busy holding onto something that you think is valuable, not knowing that that very same thing is blocking the wonderful blessings that God has in store for you.

Take control of your life bearing in mind that self-belief is a very important trait to exercise in life.

You need to believe in yourself first, before anyone else can believe in you and your potential. You need to know your worth first before anyone else can know and value your worth. You need to establish and believe in the potential that you have. That is the only way you are going to attract the right people's attention in your life.

This is because the way you portray yourself and the way you handle situations in your life are the things that people actually perceive.

It is not about how great your voice or accent is. It is about your appearance and how you carry yourself. You need to believe that you are good at something and you should try it out.

Being good at something gives a person the opportunity and platform to do better. However, the only way you can do better, is by doing your utmost best.

There comes a time in life when common sense makes no sense and when that moment comes, I often turn to science. As you know, science has very interesting and, sometimes, very difficult terms to understand. I never did well in physics, hence I opted to write.

Be that as it may, there are quite a few basic laws that I learned in physics that linger through my mind every now and again when life makes no sense to me…Netwon's laws of motion, potential energy and kinetic energy. Because I could not understand their formulas, I decided to use them theoretically, in a quest to make sense of life.

According to Newton's first law of motion, an object will remain at rest and stagnant until it is set in motion. This same law works hand-in-hand with potential energy. Potential energy in science refers to energy that is stored in a body. This is unused energy. You see in life, each and every single one of us was brought to earth, with "potential energy". This same potential that we possess is not found in the food we eat or the breast milk we drank as infants.

Instead, it is something that is inherent in all of us. We were born with it! Because we all have potential inherent in us, by default, we have the power to do something or somethings with our lives! However, it is up to us to decide whether we want to make use of that potential or not. We should also bear in mind that potential works hand-in-hand with purpose.

Now, in order for one to move from the potential energy state, kinetic energy must take place. Defined, kinetic energy simply refers to the energy that a specified object has as a result of its motion. It is also important to take note that kinetic energy does not revolve around motion only but motion as a result of mass or the force applied. In this context, the mass refers to one's hard work and effort.

This means that the acceleration of your dreams is not influenced by your words only but relies heavily on your action which is motivated by your hard work. In other words, one cannot expect to get 80% for an exam, when they only started studying the previous day. You need to put in maximum effort in order to get maximum results in life.

You have to admit that this makes sense because even Newton's third law of motion states that for every action in nature, there is an opposite and equal reaction. Therefore, you cannot say you want to become a public speaker, when the only person you feel confident speaking with- is yourself…through the mirror. You need to get out there to set your dreams in the right motion!

Even in life, no matter how much the importance of hard work is preached, there will always be those people that stubbornly stay in the state of inertia. These are people possessing a bad tendency of wanting to do absolutely nothing. These are the very same people that expect things to fall on their laps. We can all make reference to these people…Your average slay queens…People that breed children like farm animals but have no means to fend for them. A few years down the line, these same people expect the world to feel sorry for them and give them social grants and land that they are still going to misuse anyway!

We all want to have good things yet very few of us are willing to put in enough effort to get them. Everything we need to make it in life has already been given to us.

We just have to vest energy in finding our purpose and setting it in motion.

Possessing all the knowledge that I possess, I sometimes get angry when everything seems stuck. There came a point while I was compiling this book, when I realised that I may not even have the money to get it printed. And that really pissed me off because I felt that the hardest part, which was writing the book- was done.

I obviously did not expect to face more hurdles. But right now I thank God that I did not get that money then. Had I published the book then, it would have been literally ticking off publishing the book, as a goal of 2018- which was not my only goal.

I have been writing academically since I could hold a pen. However, to write my truth down, I started in grade with poetry. Nobody really cared about my writing then. And I always hid my work because people belittled the power of words and having the ability to jot them down. I wrote for myself until I completed my grade 12. It was only then that I felt confident enough to even publish a poetry book, *Reflections By Grace* alongside a motivational book, *Tribute to love.* Even then, those books never reached what I can call a solid readership.

At that point in my life, just holding my books in my hands was more than enough. However, with this particular book I wanted to go a step further, which involved helping change people's lives.

It is quite obvious that I cannot change the entire world but if I can just change a "slice" of the world with this book then I am happy. The way in which the content of this book is laid out, makes it impossible for one not to be moved at all.

So while I could not get the funds to print the book, I decided to keep refining its content. One thing I have learned about written text is that it can constantly be modified. You can imagine the amount of times I opened my manuscript, while waiting to publish it and finally get it in print…But here we are…You are reading it.

The moral of my story is that you should not fear taking risks. I had other options which included giving up on this book and waiting for someone to fund it. I could have also decided to put this book in the drawer…But I did not, instead I decided to work on it and in the end it paid off.

You see, life on its own is a gamble and I always try to make some sense of it all through analogies. This time around, I made use of the National Lottery.

In order to play the National Lottery, you need to have a Lotto bet slip which consists of numbers 1 to 52. In order to place a bet, one needs to select five numbers and then select a bonus ball. You also get to select whether you want to play the single Lotto for R5.00. To increase your chances of winning, you can play the Lotto Plus 1 and Lotto Plus 2 with an additional R2.50 for each bet. However, in order to bet the Lotto Plus 2 you have to bet the Lotto Plus 1. Thereafter, you will have to take your bet slip to a teller to make a payment of your bet.

You will then get a receipt with all the numbers that you bet. Furthermore, you will have to write your name at the back of the receipt and ensure that you retain the receipt until you receive the results of the Lotto Draw, to see whether you have won.

A lot of people place bets every week, twice a week even and very few win. Those who win the draw, win either by a stroke of luck or because they have been persistent. Now, that is how we should view life. It is interesting how the numbers on the Lotto bet slip range from 1 to 52 because it between ages 1 to 52 that we are granted the opportunity to make something out of our lives. Within these same years, we are also given enough room to make mistakes, learn from them and ultimately make the right choices.

We also need to select the bonus ball when playing the Lotto. When you have the bonus ball, you will get more money than just having three ordinary matching numbers. The irony of it all is that we all need to select a bonus ball. And in life, our bonus ball is our faith. Your bonus ball, which is your faith, is the catalyst that makes you see yourself at an advanced level, whilst you are still a beginner. It is that same faith that will turn your vision into reality. For anything good to happen in your life, you need to have faith because without faith it is very easy for your vision to become derailed.

It is also crucial for you to know and understand that faith starts with you. There is no substitute for faith. Only ignorant people can approach life without faith. You need to have faith in all that you do, in order to increase the chances of your dreams becoming a reality.

The other "five numbers" can represent your traits, the friends you keep, your goals, your approach towards life and your responsibilities...And you have to choose them well. On top of all this, it is your faith that will guarantee that you get somewhere in life.

It is up to us to decide whether we want to bet the single Lotto of R5.00 or place higher bets. Bear in mind that everyone can bet the single Lotto. So in order to be different, we have to break free from normality. If we want greater things in life, our mind-sets need to shift. Let us bet the Lotto Plus 1 in our lives so we can increase our chances of winning in this life...Let us dream bigger and try to approach life from a different perspective.

If we can get to the point of betting the Lotto Plus 1 then we can also play the Lotto Plus 2, which gives us an even greater pool of winning. So, if we want to prosper in life, we should not be afraid of increasing our bets which represent our hard work and determination.

Life is a gamble. It comes with no manual. We can try reading the Bible or the Quran but they are also very subjective. However, when all is said and done, we are the ones responsible for the outcome of our lives. We are all confronted with challenges in life…Sometimes every day.

More so, we need to choose how we react to those challenges. Our reactions to challenges are influenced by how we were raised and how we choose to allow situations to influence who we are.

This explains why when some people are faced with challenges they either, fight back or give up…And we all know what happens to those who give up. Challenges are not there to break us, they are there to help measure our growth.

In order to survive in this world, we need to have strong hearts for this world is not for the faint hearted. The keyword is "strong" because we need to be strong minded and strong willed and know what we want as soon as possible. Let us not waste our lives by chasing dead air. Let us stop giving up. This is because once we learn to give up on one thing; it becomes easy for us to give up on everything else. Let giving up on "giving up", be the only and last thing we give up on.

Let us approach life like the National Lottery ticket. Let us choose our bets, place our bets and make sure that even if we do not win that one time that next time we will try again.

Like in the National Lottery, in life we can place as many bets as we want. And because life is continuous, we should also make continuation a part of who we are. Our lives' stories can only be declared over by death. And even at that, we should make it a point that by the time our lives are over, future generations will still be able to narrate our stories. Be that as it may, it is also foolish to have faith in something that you are not passionate about. The most successful people succeed not by themselves but by the passion that drives them.

People who listen to their passion are unstoppable. You should, therefore, pace yourself on finding what you are passionate about before making any life changing decision(s). If you do what you are passionate about, no recession or hurdle will let your passion die. Once you have found what you are passionate about, work on it, invest in it and have faith in it. If you do not have faith in yourself, there is no way you will have faith in seeing your vision become a success. When you have a dream or vision that you want to actualize, you need to be positive minded at all times. It should not even matter whether you have the funds to execute your plan or not, just always keep your "end product" in mind.

We are all hungry for success. And it is only our passion, faith and positive thoughts that can feed that hunger. Fortunately, those things are free of charge.

However, we should also remember that with the same passion, faith and positive thoughts comes hard work!

Knowing Love

Love…

Back in the day, love was everywhere; it was literally in the air. A person would look at the other and tell them they loved them and actually meant it. Well, my dear, it is just too bad that some of us were not born during that era. All that we have are songs by the likes of Michael Jackson and Luther Vandross to remind us of how great love used to be back then.

Do not get me wrong, but even today we still listen to old school music. Not because it is just music but because it is rooted and has a lot of meaning. That is why those musicians are called legends…Because the message they send across about love is strong and pure. Let us take Michael Jackson's song titled *Speechless* for example. It is a remarkable song.

Again, do not get me wrong, but when last did you hear a lady or gentleman say to you "Speechless that's how you make me feel" (Sony/ATV Music Publishing LLC) or "I'd rather have bad times with you, than good times with someone else" (I'd Rather lyrics © Universal Music Publishing Group)?

Oh and how can we forget the ladies in the music industry that make love stay true, like the late Whitney Houston and the remarkable lady, Toni Braxton? If you doubt me, listen to *Worth it* by Whitney from her last album and the hit song *Rollercoaster* by Toni Braxton featuring Baby Face. In *Rollercoaster,* Toni Braxton explains how love is like a rollercoaster that is always going up and down. So if you thought love is supposed to remain in one place, then you better listen to that song.

Besides that song, God was not a fool when He said love holds no record of wrongs, in the book of Corinthians (1 Corinthians 13 NIV). He specifically stated it because love's hands are supposed to be so full of the right things that it should not carry any wrong. Does this make sense?

Fortunately and unfortunately in this generation, every time we get into a relationship we literally hope that "This time it is love". We go from one relationship to the next all in the quest to find love. Although we go through a series of relationships, we have got to admire the fact that we do not give up. We may get to the finish line, which is marriage, tired but in the end, we do get there. We want marriage so bad…against all odds, with or without the ring!

Now that part is wrong with our generation. We tend to worry more about what the public spectacle has to say about our lives, especially regarding whether we get married or not. Unfortunately, not everyone is destined to get married. The statistics have even proved that there are more women in the world than men. We can still try polygamy but still not everyone will find a suitor and that would increase the death toll anyway. If marriage is not for you, it is just not for you. So you can tell your family members to relax a bit. And besides, you do not need marriage to validate your existence.

Any way whether you want to believe me or not, the truth is that lately, instead of *love* being the opposite of *lust, love* has become a synonym of *lust*. If love lasts forever, then lust should be temporary, right? To illustrate my point of love being synonymous with lust,

I am going to tell you something that you might have not been aware of or chose to ignore until now.

So many couples get married and in a few years, if not months, they get divorced. We can all make references of failed marriages, you, me and the person beside you… Why is that? The answer is simple- They got divorced because they had no love for one another, instead they only had an idea of what love is and could be like- full stop! People do not get divorced because of infidelity, abuse, or financial changes. If you serve the living God and you genuinely love your partner, you will not simply give up on him because he has lost his job or you saw him with a "potential threat". Hey, listen, you communicate with God and your partner. In this process you should also bear in mind that love conquers all- only through patience and having faith.

Do not come here with your features of an ideal partner or what worked in your grandparents' marriage!

Acknowledge this; you will get tests in life. Tests do not just end in school; they are everywhere in life. The nice thing about tests is that they help you grow. Without tests you cannot grow mentally and emotionally. At work there are written warnings… Even in your personal life you get confronted by weight gain for example. You will then have to choose whether you are going to exercise to trim that fat or you are going to live with it and risk obesity and other possible dread diseases. So I ask… Why should there not be any tests in your relationship? This world is very crude; it is either you are strong or you are out!

While at the quest of finding love we should also learn to get rid of expectations.

At times when we step into relationships, we come with a checklist of the things we expect from the people we say we love and want to build a future with. We come into relationships with our sets of boundaries in our subconscious. However, we forget that we said that we love them. When you say you love someone, you say so based on how you feel. When you acknowledge that you love someone, you do so voluntarily. How you treat the person that you say you love should correspond with the way you "claim" to feel about him or her. In essence, when you say you love someone, it is just you saying how that person makes you feel. And how you make that person feel could be completely different.

Learn to get rid of expectations when you get into a relationship. Things will happen the way that they should happen.

Somehow, it makes sense why we already have the dos and don'ts when we get into relationships. The pains of our past relationships have made our minds formulate that "checklist" because we don't want to go through such pain again. However, this fear brings more pain than joy. The fear of your current relationship turning out like your previous relationship becomes a reality because you are thinking too much about it. Let the past remain in the past.

When we expect certain behaviours from our partners, we often set traps of offence. Take, for example, when you call your partner and he does not respond to your call or get back to you, like you do when he calls you…What happens next? You automatically become offended and disappointed and all of a sudden, that one "failed expectation" erases all the good that your partner has brought into your life. All of this happens because your expectation was not met. This clearly shows that we need to get rid of expectations when we step into relationships.

Do something because you want to do it and not because you need approval from another person. It goes without saying that living without being offended once in a while is almost impossible but it could happen a lot less, if we learned to get rid of expectations.

There is also this thing about love...If we had to define love, every individual would have his or her own definition of what love is. There is absolutely nothing wrong with that. I would like to believe that everyone has got their own definition of love because of how love manifests in their own lives. It is allowed...

You have the right to envision love the way you see it through your own eyes. After all, when you say you love somebody, you say so because of what you feel for that person.

I am going to share some tips regarding love with you. Firstly, learn to be careful of love. The same way love makes you strong is the same way it can make you weak. Unfortunately, it is not all the time that we are able to find balance in love. When all is said and done love is still beautiful but dangerous at the same time.

The only way you can monitor and sustain the degree of the love you have for your significant other is by having an intimate relationship with God with all your heart and allowing His love to manifest in your life first before you can love another. People often say "God is love" and whether you want to believe it or not, God is really love.

Once you involve God in your relationship, things will work out maybe for better or worse. You can pray for God's direction in your relationship and things blossom in it. You may also pray for God to bless your union and you end up separating with your partner. If it does happen that you break up with your partner, it does not mean that you were not praying hard enough. Nor does it mean that God does not love you. Just take it as God telling you that your relationship was not going to get any better hence things ended the way they did.

Pray for your partner. Pray for God to direct you and the relationship you are involved in. Once you start praying, ask God to show you the signs whether your partner is the one. Get this; the "one" does not have to be your husband or wife. You need to ask God whether your current partner is the one that will make and help you grow and give you enough experience so that you can make it in marriage and life in general, one day. Once you get to see the signs, do not ignore them. God will show you through certain things if your partner is not the one for you. Remember this; God does not want His children to get hurt. And we should also not allow ourselves to get hurt due to our ignorance and stubbornness.

You also need to acknowledge that love consists of a spiritual and realistic connection. A spiritual connection is simple; you go down on your knees and say "God, I have seen someone and I would like to believe that I love him or her as my partner. But God because I am Your child and I have humanly eyes, help me see whether he or she is the one. Amen."

A realistic connection in love is also pretty much simple. A realistic connection in a relationship revolves around you having the ability to acknowledge that fights and mistakes are there. Most importantly, you need to learn that forgiveness is key.

Unfortunately, forgiveness is often the saddest and most emotionally draining journey that one can ever go through in life. This is because when you find yourself at a point where you have to forgive someone, it means that you actually acknowledge and accept that this person has wronged you. Bear in mind that if a person wrongs you, it means that your trust for that person is affected. And because your trust in that person is affected, you slowly stop believing in that person. When you trust someone, it means that you have faith that that particular person will not let you down.

So the fact that you became offended by the "act" of your offender means that you did not expect such behaviour from that person. The moment you get to the point of forgiveness, you as the wronged one should, first of all, forgive yourself.

Often, when people wrong us we subconsciously feel that we are hurt because we chose to let these people into our lives and actually put our trust in them voluntarily. We tend to shift the blame from the people who offended us to ourselves automatically. As a result, we think that we are not worthy of love in any form of relationship or friendship- which is wrong.

We do not just let anybody into our lives if they do not even add a strand of value to our lives.

This explains why the people that we have allowed into our lives have an even greater advantage to offend us over mere strangers.

I always say that one never knows a person until they know a person. It is only when people put you in a box and you start to relax that you get to see them for who they really are. Most of the time, these people are boom slangs that appear as bush snakes. It is, unfortunately, only when they bite you that you actually feel the toxicity of their venom. You, therefore, have to be careful of these people. However, if you find yourself bitten by these people, you should just forgive yourself.

Forgiveness does not just occur. It takes a lot of thought processing more especially from you, the offended one.

Therefore, when you decide to forgive someone you should not do so for the sake of doing so. You can only do so after you have thought through the depth of the offence.

I like to view offence from two stances; the primary offence and the secondary offence. The primary offence refers to the simple offences such as someone missing your calls and not getting back to you… And of course getting blue ticked. As light as these offences are, they are often the catalysts to secondary offences and should therefore not be disregarded. The secondary offences are offences committed by the ones close to us. These are offences committed by people that actually know us and the things that can literally throw us off! Once someone commits a secondary offence, you will have to sit down and think whether this person offended you intentionally or unintentionally. It is only once you think through whether the person offended you intentionally or unintentionally that you will be able to conclude and know what you mean to that person. An unintentional offence can easily be defined as the first offence…When you and this person are trying to get to know each other and he or she "unintentionally" offends you.

Most of the time when we initiate relationships and friendships, we base the foundation of our "ships" on words. It is only as time goes by, that we are able to detect whether our words are coherent with our actions. This explains why these unintentional offences occur. However, it is the intentional offences that make us pull out the red card. If people do exactly what you told them you do not like repetitively - even after you cautioning them, that is an intentional offence.

You can still forgive these people. But this time around, you should set boundaries in your heart and mind for these people.

At the end of the day, because you are the one faced with this offence, you are ought to initiate the forgiveness process and it can only work out well if it starts with you. Always remember that how people treat you has got nothing to do with you, but is just a mere reflection of who they are. With that being said, the relationships that last and survive for years are the ones that have endurance, patience, faith and forgiveness.

You also need to make peace with some things because if you do not, they will crush you and swallow you. Cheating is unfortunately there. I am not condoning it, nor am I saying that you should conform to it. All I am saying is that you should just accept that it is there.

It has always been there. Even Bathsheba cheated on her husband with David in the Bible.

Cheating has different degrees in which we take it or perceive it. A lot of people break up because they caught their partners in bed with another person. Fortunately and unfortunately that is not the only form of cheating. Being secretive, hiding your money, hiding your true feelings about something, deleting conversations or images you feel might hurt your partner…that is also cheating. The minute you do something that you know your partner does not like or will not like, you should know that you are already cheating.

So what I am saying is simple; mistakes, cheating and fights are there. Things will only and always work out if the wrong partner acknowledges his or her faults and asks for forgiveness.

However, the wronged one must also have the ability to forgive the wrong one. Do not be proud by trying to prolong an argument. You are not perfect and the day shall come when you will be caught up in the same or similar situation. Forget your ego and hunger for revenge when you want to work things out in your relationship.

Once you are careful of love, you need to appreciate it. Appreciate love.

Unfortunately, in the era we live in, our love has a breaking point, whereby we get fed up and just want to quit. Overall, every single thing in life has a limit and if you exceed the limit or get below the minimum level, you can get hurt. That is why we need to learn to love love and to appreciate and cherish it.

Love may have its flaws but it can complete you. If you take care of love, love will take care of you. Whether we like it or not we need love in our lives.

We need to appreciate love because not everyone is exposed to it. Some people hate themselves so much and resort to using drugs as an emotional escape or get exposed to abuse because they have no love. Do not make foolish mistakes that might make you lose your loved one. And because love does not give up, you should also not give up on it.

Do not involve your friends in your relationship. Do not involve your family in your relationship. If you have a problem, talk to your significant other, not your family or friends. Acknowledge this; your family and friends are only there as your support system and they serve as ears to your problems but your partner is there to understand you.

Once you have become careful of love and started appreciating it, you still need to maintain it. Love needs maintenance. A relationship is like a new born baby; in fact treat it like a new born baby.

A child starts as a new born which becomes an infant that progresses to a toddler and so forth. Such is a relationship. Realistically speaking, you cannot breastfeed a child till he or she is ten years old! Nature does not allow that! Therefore, you cannot rely on applying the same methods you used when the relationship was fresh into another phase of your relationship.

If you do so, your relationship will not grow and it will remain stagnant. That is why you will find that people have been dating for seven years yet there is no marriage.

This happens because they are not allowing their relationship to grow. You will also find that a couple has been together for over three years, yet the one partner is still insecure. Believe me you do get such people. And that is utterly wrong. Listen- because you are still insecure in your long relationship, learning to trust your partner will never be easy and it will take time. And let us be honest, a relationship needs some level of trust for it to work.

So, in simple terms, you should just always ensure that you never carry your personal insecurities into a relationship because they will hinder the progress of your relationship.

Love is very delicate; you need to feed it well so that it can grow well.

I once wrote a poem called *Tea Time* that can be found in my poetry book, *Reflections by Grace*.

>Love is not a bed of roses
>
>Love has different poses
>
>Filled with good and bad doses
>
>Your heart is like a cup
>
>Filled with boiling water to the brim
>
>All the way up
>
>The tea bag is added

This tea covers disappointments

If you do not ensure that you remove the tea bag in time

Your tea will be too strong and bitter for you to drink

Add some sugar to make your relationship sweet

Though adding too much of it might push your partner away

You can add some milk to increase the happiness

Make sure it is still fresh to avoid sadness

Lastly stir your relationship to be the way you want it to be

Then drink it while it's still warm

Because no one would want to drink cold tea

As much as no one would want to stay in a relationship

that is cold

Love is a feeling that only a few believe in

But it is experienced, because of the world we live in

All that counts is what you

Believe in

It is a simple and straight forward poem, just elaborating on love through a cup of tea that everyone is familiar with. The nice thing with the symbolism I created with a cup of tea, is that it makes love seem very unique and easy. Like love, tea is essential. It keeps you warm during winter and during summer you may hate it but once in a while you cannot help but to drink it. That is love. There are times when you heavily depend on it…

And sometimes you may feel like you do not need it but you end up keeping it anyway…

Because it makes you happy. However, love can only make you happy if you put yourself first. This is because once you put yourself first, you are able to put things in your mind and process them by yourself. You also get the ability to weigh your options. Most importantly, the end result will be the one that suits you and makes you happy. When you put yourself first you become less likely to get hurt because you are handling your life your own way. However, you will also have to adjust your life if you want to accommodate someone else in your life.

Often at times people say you should not change your ways in order to sustain a relationship. Oh and if you do try to change, people say it is not love. So I ask, what is a relationship?

Here is the thing; you cannot make a relationship work on your own. It is called a relationship because it needs to involve two partners – at least. One of the many factors that are key to making a relationship work involve having the ability to sacrifice, having the ability to compromise and building trust.

I need you to know that there is a difference between changing in order to ensure that a relationship works and changing so much that your life solely depends and revolves around your relationship and partner. When you change so that a relationship can work, it means no longer spending every second you have with your friends but dividing your time in such a way that it accommodates your partner.

People do not realize that a relationship needs a lot of work. Hey, that thing is a lot of work!

Bearing that in mind, you cannot build a relationship over the phone, e-mails or WhatsApp. Computer-mediated technology just serves as a catalyst for your relationship's growth. With that being said you cannot build a relationship without intimate communication. A relationship needs communication and time.

So now, imagine that you are in a relationship with a person that calls you maybe twice a week. Believe me when I tell you that if your partner cannot make time for you then the existence of your relationship is nothing more than a figment of your imagination.

Learn to put yourself first. Do not lose yourself in love. Love is about having someone in your life as a "part" of your life and not dominating your entire life.

When I talk about a person being a part of your life, I actually mean your partner having a certain segment in your life. You still need to be able to do things on your own. You still need to breathe. You still need to think on your own, have your goals and also focus on your career.

The mistake that people often make is that they pray for love, they get the love, they maintain their relationships but then lose themselves in their relationships. As a result, their identities become profound in their relationships and marriages. Hence, when things are going astray in their relationships, their whole lives become affected. You do not maintain love by just remaining stagnant in it.

When you get into a relationship you need to ensure that that same person you are involved with allows you to grow in that relationship, and vice versa.

It is true that love is about sacrifices but you get people that want to sacrifice their whole lives for a relationship and their relationship gets doomed... Too much of a good thing is bad. When you do such things you push love away. Once you start thinking that you are sacrificing too much, you need to stop and watch if your partner is doing the same. If you are sacrificing alone, you will end up living for another person and not for yourself.

Once you lose yourself in love, you are going to lose your identity completely. You need to take care of love so that love can take care of you. People go mad because of love. People use love potions to get love.

People die because of love. And people kill in the name of love. Hey, love is dangerous! It is saddening that as a matter of fact all of us never really know whether the people we love actually love us. We hear them say they love us and all we can do, is just wait for them to put their love into action.

You can find a person that claims to love you so much. You will then end up believing that this person loves you because of the role this person plays…Then one day you find out that the same person is unfaithful to you. Sad neh?! Let me tell you something, "That has nothing to do with you". Whether he or she cheated on you or whether he or she was not genuine to you has absolutely nothing to do with you. Continue playing your role as a man or woman in your relationship. If the person fails to stay true to you, they are actually failing themselves…

It is their loss, not yours. Fulfil your role as a man or woman and have forgiveness. You need to forgive.

You need to have the ability to forgive because love has understanding and it is not perfect. I will constantly mention forgiveness because it is important. Most, if not all crimes of passion occur as a result of lack of acceptance and lack of forgiveness. I therefore urge you to practice forgiveness, not for the other person but for yourself.

When you came to earth you saw what you desire for your future and set the goals you want to achieve. Carry on working on those goals. Do not put your life at a standstill for someone who can leave you at any minute. If you loved a person, if you loved someone whole heartedly, once that person leaves you, you are going to get deeply hurt. It is expected.

However, you need to be happy about one thing; that you did not disappoint them. I cannot even begin to imagine carrying all the hurt and bitterness towards myself because I hurt someone who actually valued me…Imagine!

Love is a very difficult emotion to comprehend. Love is also a very important and complex subject that a lot of psychologists and the Bible itself have tried to simplify. But this is life…All we can do is hope that we can help each other and heal one another by sharing our experiences.

Letting Go

As people we conduct ourselves differently, hence some people find it easier to move on after a break up than others. Women have been proven to be more emotional than men; which explains why we find moving on after a break up as a scientific assignment with no solution. We cry, till no tears come out, eat ice cream, watch movies... The list is endless. We all have different methods of dealing with break ups with hopes to find good results, after all. The naked truth is that no one wants to dwell in self-pity all their lives long simply because one individual disappointed them.

It is expected that everyone will start picturing themselves walking down the aisle with their partners- I mean that is the whole purpose of a relationship after all. However, the sad thing is that we often find it that only one partner is more committed and serious about the relationship, while the other one is just fooling around or trying to find his or her feet. I would like to believe that it is unfair because it is like you are deceiving and misleading the other person.

There was a time in my life, when I thought that many relationships undergo such experiences because they do not tell each other what they want and expect from one another from the start…Then 2018 came along, ha! These days, people will tell you that they will be good to you, treat you well blah blah blah and then go AWOL. Hey they will leave you with no sign, no notice and no fights!

What then? What do you do when you get caught up in such a situation?

Well, I learned that we cannot change other people but we can learn to change how we respond to the way they treat us. At the end of the day, everything does come to an end. Obviously, when you are with someone, it is because you feel something for that person. And once that person leaves, notice or no notice, it will hurt. Come to think of it… If losing that person does not hurt, then what you felt for him or her was probably not real.

Given we cannot know how people truly feel about us, we have to rely on extracting what we feel we want from them for as long as they are still with us.

Do this so that when that person decides to leave you, you will know that at least you were able to feel a certain way. This will not make you feel or seem needy. Instead, it will give you, at least some level of fulfilment.

When you find yourself at a place where you have to let go, please do not become angry with yourself. Please do not become bitter…Well, it is okay to become sad. But in the midst of all that pain and sadness, just take a moment and just remember what you shared with that person. Treasure how you felt when you were with that person… The good times of course. Be happy that at least you were able to feel how love can make one feel.

The other thing that kills people is getting into relationships because they want to avoid being alone. Others get into relationships just to "fit in" so that when their friends talk about their partners, they also have someone to talk about. If you are getting into a relationship because of that, then my dear friend you are entering into a relationship for the wrong reasons.

When you want a partner, you look for a person that possesses the qualities that you want in a man and not just because he is a guy that is single and you are also single. It does not work like that! I would advise you to be patient with love; otherwise you will keep meeting people that are not meant for you.

Now, the thing that happens almost all the time is comparison amongst friends. When a friend becomes single, the one who is still in a relationship will either start acting weird towards her friend… Or the "now single" friend will start feeling lesser than the friend who is still in a relationship.

Listen, just because your friend has a successful relationship does not mean that because you broke up with your partner you will not have a successful relationship. Remember this; you are you.

You are unique. Your destiny has been planned in a different way as compared to that of your friends'.

If you want to have a good relationship, start with a good foundation. And always remember that a successful relationship takes time, sacrifices and commitment. If you do not have those features then you should not even bother trying to get into a relationship.

The truth hurts but just has to be told. Most of us assume that we are in relation"ships" whilst we are in relation"boats". By so saying; we invest our time and efforts in "good for nothing" relationships. If that partner of yours does not make sacrifices, expects you to check up on him and run after him like a demented dog… Why even bother carrying on with that relationboat? Stop deceiving yourself and do not allow him to deceive you in the process. Strays belong to no one.

No one said letting go is easy but it will do you a lot of good if you step out of a relationship that can harm you emotionally.

I have formulated the basic steps of letting go of a relationship successfully.

These steps include knowing that it is not your fault, it's his loss, accepting the locus and being determined to let go. These steps also touch on getting rid of what's his, letting the pain out, asking for social support and the importance of forgiveness.

Step 1: It is not your fault

Most women blame themselves when their relationships are no longer good. They always excuse the man from the picture and blame themselves for their partners' failure to play their roles in their relationships. Well, it is in fact about time you stopped blaming yourself for everything. Do not play the "victim". Never do it because it will consume you and kill your soul.

Start looking at your man and whether he fulfilled his roles as your partner. Study whether he was a good man- the one that you wanted or at least thought you wanted. Even if it means taking a pen and paper to note all the good and bad things he has done to you, do it! You might think that it is unnecessary but it is actually helpful because it will help you realise whether you are in a healthy relationship or not. An unhealthy relationship is not good for you because it is not healthy for goodness sake. Relationships have an effect on our psychological well-being.

Therefore, being in an unhealthy relationship then becomes detrimental for our psyche. Now, I would go on and on, trying to explain the psychological effects of a bad relationship on a person but I would bore you. Have you ever wondered why some women undergo severe emotional breakdowns when their relationships are no more? Most certainly you have seen women crying over relationships, undergoing stress, going through depression and being admitted to psychiatric centres. Newsflash: If you continue staying in an unhealthy relationship, you will also be a part of those women.

It therefore becomes your responsibility as a woman to know when to let go. It is your responsibility to also know that you are not guilty (if you are not).

If you know that "you" have been trying to make the relationship work, then you have been wasting your time. In order for a relationship to work both partners need to be involved, not just you. So stop saying you are going to try to be a better woman…Both of you should try being better partners to one another!

Some women often complain, saying that their partners take them for granted. I am also one of these women. This usually happens when you are trying to make a sinking relationship remain above water. If your partner does not help maintain the relationship; it is either he is maintaining another relationship with someone else or you have become a complete bore in his life. However, it is not your fault.

I also know that as women we tend to try hard to please our partners. There is absolutely nothing wrong with that. However, when he does not do anything to make you feel like a woman, then it becomes something that is totally wrong and unacceptable. The main purpose of being in a relationship is being with someone who supports you emotionally, someone who does not judge you but makes you feel special instead.

When you step into a relationship, you and your partner must become each other's anchors by default. You must have that assurance that you can rely on and trust your partner and vice versa. A relationship requires the willingness of both partners to make it work. If the one partner is not doing his part then the relationship is going to crumble. Do not stay in a relationship that might end up destroying your chances of being happy in life.

If you are going through a break up you should know that you and your partner failed to do your duties. You should also know that you are not the only one to blame.

Do not dwell in self-pity because of one break up. One bad break up does not mean that all your relationships will turn out to be the same. However, before you step into another relationship, I think you should find out what it is that you want in a man. Also try to make sense of what you could have done wrong in your past relationship so you can avoid those mishaps in future.

Step 2: It's his loss

Men are funny these days; they dump women via a phone call, SMS, Facebook, WhatsApp…

Hey ku rough! Most of the time, they will dump you without a valid reason which is rather not nice and low from them. These days you are even lucky if they tell you or text you that it is over!

I do not know about you but I believe that a real man would come to you and tell you the hard truth face to face, the same way he was able to ask you out. In most cases you will find that you have been dumped for another girl who does not even have class or standards (slay queen). You know what?! Screw him for choosing her over you. Instead of you feeling sorry for losing him, feel sorrier for him.

Yes, it is going to be hard to admit that you have been played and emotionally misused. But hey, you also need to know that we're not meant to be with a person that sees your meekness as a weakness.

Please do me a favour... Do not feel bitter because the feeling only tends to make one's life harder. Long term bitterness leads to hatred and hatred leads to anger and you do not want it, trust me. You will turn into a psycho! You are always going to think of your ex, which is unnecessary and so not good for your health. It is just not worth it.

If you really played a good part in your relationship in a matter of a few months, if not weeks, he will start bugging you and asking for your forgiveness. You may forgive him but be careful when deciding what to do next.

I have always been fascinated by snakes and for some reason, I feel it is good to use them as an analogy every once in a while... Especially in relation to matters of the heart.

Love, marriage and relationships like most snakes -are venomous. So when your partner leaves you, you are bound to feel the wrath of his or her bite, which represents his or her sudden absence in your life. The only antidote you will have will be letting go of the pain he put you through. You will also need to remain hopeful and faithful that you will find someone who will appreciate your very existence.

Now, when this snake decides to come back and invade your home, there are a few things you can do;

- (a) Try to chase the snake away nicely by swearing at it. Tell your ex "I do not want to be with you anymore because you left me and I would never have done that to you".
- (b) Kill this snake to ensure that it does not come back into your life ever again. By this I do not

mean that you should murder your ex! Just sit down with your ex and make him or her see the facts of your separation. One of these facts being not only that he left but because he left you to make sense of the baseless foundation he made you lay your heart on.

(c) Take the snake back in. The advantage of this option is that at least you will know how this snake operates. This snake will know that no matter how much it tries to gain your trust fully again, that this time around you will have a shield protecting you from its bite(s).

If you know that you fulfilled your duties as a girlfriend and woman to your partner… If you know you did your part to sustain the relationship, then you have absolutely no reason to beg him to stay with you. I mean, you have done all that you could… Does that make sense?

Do not even bug him once he has left. If you bug him (knowing some of these men), you are going to make him happy as it will be clear that he still has power over you. Leave him alone because in order to be able to handle rejection, you have to go through rejection.

Some will say that if you have a baby with the partner it is a different story. Sure it is, but a baby is not a ticket to marriage nor does it secure your chances of being with a man. In fact, a baby is most likely going to bring the cracks of your relationship to the surface rather than repair them. There are many, and I mean many, single mothers out there who are successful, surviving and happy with their children, join them. The Almighty God will give you strength to raise your child(ren).

Step 3: Accept the locus

If he does not want to be with you any longer, there is pretty much nothing you can do to change that situation. No amount of explanations or reasoning can change his mind.

However, should you choose to stay with him, you should know that you chose to be alone. But I ask "Why would you choose to carry a candle without a flame"? I remember when I chose to stick with a "dead" relationship. Believe me, it was never nice! He continued to torture me way more than he ever did. He started flirting with other women. He actually cared less about how I felt and what I thought about what he was doing. As if that was not enough, he started giving me conditions in the relationship. He told me when to call and when not to call.

He judged me and made me feel incompetent. I had no power over him, to the extent that I became dependent on his cold-heartedness towards me. It was like he dominated my very existence! I cried almost every day. This man was an onion in my life! I went through a lot of unnecessary stress which led to a drop in my school performance and I no longer had a social life.

All those things happened because I did not accept that we were over from the start. I held onto a failed relationship, trying to work things out. In the end it turned out to be a waste of my time and tears. What I went through was just unbelievable. I was weak and lacked control over my life but had I accepted that it was over when he told me so, I would not have gone through what I went through. I sometimes look at myself through the mirror and simply cannot believe that I put myself under so much torture for a person that I did not even need.

Step 4: Be determined to let go

If you feel you are not ready to let go, do not let go. Often at times, we will leave our partners because we were angry at that moment.

Later on, once we have calmed down we regret what we said and why we left. Packing a suitcase can take you around thirty minutes on a normal day… But when you are fed up with your partner, all you need is two minutes and then you are done! By so saying, I mean that you should not leave a person if you know that you are not over him or her yet because you are going to make things rather difficult for yourself.

Take for example when you are eating your favourite cake. You would not want to throw it away until it is finished. However, the only reasons you would throw it away is if it has expired or if it starts to taste bad. The same applies with a relationship. If you like the person you are with you should not let go until you are ready to do so.

Even if he is giving you signs that he is over you, do not leave him unless you are over him as well. Imagine you are having your favourite meal with your partner and all of a sudden he decides he is full. He then expects you to also stop eating because he is done eating…In the meantime; you are still enjoying your meal! That is pure selfishness! Hey, he must wait until you finish your meal as well. Give him a toothpick while you also get done eating!

It becomes easier to lose feelings for a person who is no longer playing his role in the relationship. The feelings you had for him will start decrease perhaps on daily or weekly basis. It all depends on how determined you are about letting go of the whole relationship.

What I am also aware of, is the fact that it is easy to let go of a relationship but it is difficult to let go of your partner. Surely, I do not expect you to forget about him the minute you leave him. Instead, all I am saying is that you can easily forget about the relationship but not your partner.

In my situation it took me four months to admit that he was no longer mine to keep and that he was no longer a part of my life. During those four months things were hard for me but good for him. I would see him laughing, smiling and all jolly while I was in fact feeling the opposite. Do you feel my frustration at that time though? Whenever I saw him, I felt all bitter and angry because he was cheating on me.

On top of that, he never really explained what I had done to him that was so bad that he even resorted to treating me like I meant nothing to him. This was in 2011 and if you remember very well, during that period, cheating was a taboo. So when he cheated on me, I was offended and things just ended abruptly. You see around 2010-2013 you would easily get an explanation from your partner for cheating and a sincere apology…Not these days!

The truth is that after the four months of self-recovery and self-discovery, I felt really good and finally forgave him. We started interacting casually like normal friends, which I think he did not like.

When he saw and heard that I was doing better without him he started bugging me, asking me to give him another chance. Basically every ex or former lover is like that. When they see that you are doing better without them, they do not like it. It is like they want us to suffer but what counts is your determination of letting go.

Your friends may also advise you time and time again and over and over again to dump your partner. Hello- you will not leave your partner if you are not ready to do so! People might think that you are a fool but you are not. Love can make you lose your intelligence because when you are under the impulse of affection you are capable of doing crazy things. However, once you start letting go whilst you are in the relationship you are actually regaining your intelligence.

You also become easily aware of the things you may have taken for granted while you were still blinded by what you believed was love. So do not worry about people's opinions. Do what you feel is right for you.

Friends- I do not hate them, I love them but sometimes they mislead us. It is quite obvious that once you are hurt you will run to your friends for support. Actually, that is the time you will need them the most. However, you need to be careful of them. Your friends will often tell you to let him go because he does not deserve you and that he is using you… Those assumptions could be true but the other truth is that, they do not know what you and your partner have been through together. That is why you and only you can decide whether you want to let go or not.

Some friends will say that he is not the one for you when they do not even have partners themselves...Some of them are even foreign to serious relationships! I remember this one friend of mine; I was close with her during high school. She never really liked my boyfriend and when we were fighting, she would encourage me to let him go. "Is that support? Is there a perfect relationship on earth?"

I would ask her those questions and she would fail to answer me. She also told me that she could not wait to witness the day I come to her with my eyes swollen from crying. I was disappointed. Well, I suppose I did not know how to choose my friends. That is a lesson for you too, my dear... Learn to choose the right friends and also learn to be the right friend to others.

Always remember that what and how you feel inside is what counts. It does not matter how many times people may judge you and say you are a fool and that your partner is using you. Do not listen to them. You will even find that some people enjoy seeing you in pain. But do not worry about them; they are the ones that need love the most.

When you feel it is time to let go, you will let go. Take your time; you do not need to rush. A "good" friend of mine once said to me "Girl, you know what is best for you, not me hey. But do not waste your time on non-progressive matters. Take your time and think really deep on whether you want him in your life or not. We cannot protect our own hearts, yet we want to protect other people's hearts-the very same ones who hurt us.

Do me a favour: try to be honest with yourself, you are no longer in high school."

That was award winning advice. Till today, I respect my friend. Her words were harsh but true. After that, I thought deep and I realized that my partner was just not worth it any longer. He was like a Zim Dollar; I could not do much with him. So I decided to just hang the towel but it took me time, I mean months to actually do so.

Step 5: Get rid of what's his

Check this: How many times have you tried to call your ex, even though you knew very well that you were no longer together? I know… It has happened to me a couple of times. All that I got back was either "Don't call me again, you know we are over" or they would not even pick up my calls. The worst thing was to find out that they actually blocked my numbers…This life is hard I tell you!

All those things; trying to rekindle a dead flame, were just a waste of time. Imagine blowing wind to a dead fire planning to keep yourself warm with it…Now you trying to contact your former partner is the same thing.

Unfortunately the only thing that trying to reconnect with your ex does is draw you back, disturbing your healing process. Of course it is never going to be easy to let go. Who ever said it is easy to let go, is most probably not over her ex and is still nagging him trying to reconnect with him.

If you want a way to hurt yourself over and over again, keep calling your ex. No matter how many times you try to call and explain yourself to your ex he is never going to take you back. If he does take you back, he is only going to use you- that's all! Tough luck! It is just the way it is. The truth is that while you are busy holding on to your ex, he might be holding someone else in his arms at that very moment.

When you want to let go, getting rid of contacts is probably the hardest yet efficient thing to do. By contacts, social networks are also included.

But guys, there are some women...like myself (in the past) who would log on Facebook and check their ex's wall. If you are doing that you are only hurting yourself, trust me, I know. The saddest thing is finding out he is doing quite well without you while you are not. Like I said, it is not going to be easy but it is worth it. I do not want other women to go through what I went through.

When my boyfriend let go of me, I went through a serious emotional breakdown. The reason for my emotional breakdown was not as a result of the end of our relationship…It was because the signs were there that he was going to leave me earlier, but I chose to take them for granted. I would try to call him but he would ignore my calls like I never meant anything to him. I would send him texts and he would not bother texting me back. So I made a stupid mistake.

One day, I decided to log on my Facebook account and tried to access his wall but hey, he blocked me on his Facebook. This, by default, showed that he had something to hide from me. I then took my mother's cell phone and created a Facebook account using her cell phone numbers. It was around 23:45 on a Friday night during April 2012 and I was in the kitchen.

So I finally got to his wall. To my surprise he was "engaged" to another woman. I was so devastated that I just sat on the dustbin. I could not cry but my heart was very heavy, I could barely breathe. I then in boxed him "I can see that you took my meekness towards you as a weakness". After that, I got up and went to bed but still, I could not sleep. I just thought of how he used me and the amount of times he fooled me, making me believe that I was the one for him. Still, I kept on calling him, not because I wanted him back but because I wanted an explanation... These days they call it "closure". Even though I could see that he had moved on with someone else, I still sought for an explanation. If he could tell me why he did what he did to me, most probably I would have had peace.

Instead he couldn't have cared less about how I felt. And so I had to let go the hard way- "With a bitter heart".

Getting rid of the contacts is one thing but getting rid of the memories is another! After a break up the hardest thing ever, is getting rid of the memories...Starting with pictures! I remember I had a lot of images of my boyfriend and getting rid of them was one heavy problem. I had his pictures in my room and they somehow gave my room some colour. So getting rid of them was difficult and keeping them was also very painful. One day I just told myself that I just have to get rid of them. But I did not know how to get rid of them: "Should I throw them away, tear them into pieces or burn them?" I kept asking myself those questions. I slept over those questions.

I then woke up past midnight, took those pictures, tore them into pieces and burnt them. It sounds easy but I cried. The next morning, I looked at the frame that once contained his pictures and it looked so empty. I ended up putting it away.

There is a poem that motivated me throughout my break up is called: *Too much a woman*

> I believed in you
>
> When you weren't worth believing in
>
> Stood tall
>
> By your spineless changes of character
>
> I was insane to search for sense in your craziness
>
> A foundation on shifting winds

Our memories are forgettable

You were never there to create them

Am not crying nor do I want you back

My tears are not for wasting

I left our room empty

Lose my numbers

Erase all memory

You never knew me

You tarnished my reputation

I am not weak

I was too much a woman for you

And you know it

The words of this poem helped a lot. They actually motivated me. So you can also use the poem as some sort of remedy during your recovery after a bad break up…

And then of course- the gifts. The most emotional part of letting go of the memories is because it was all nice when you got them. I do not know about you but for me, keeping the memories felt like hell. They reminded me of the good times we had which were contradictory to the bad times I was actually experiencing.

If he bought me a perfume I would hit it hard against the wall and throw away the broken glasses.

Any clothing material- I burnt it with paraffin! Here is the trick. The method you use to get rid of the memories will either destroy you or destroy the memories. If you are all sissy, honouring and caressing the object, it will destroy you emotionally. However, if you just take the object like a wild woman, chances of you feeling sad are one out of ten. By destroying them you are taking out the bitterness, sadness and hatred that you are probably feeling towards your former partner.

I do not believe in keeping things of my former lover if what we had has lapsed…Unless if it is a car…Now that I would keep!

Step 6: Let the pain out

What kills people most, figuratively and literally, after a break up is not losing the partner. It is the fact that they avoid letting the pain out. Hey, you are not a doll. We do not expect you to be completely fine after a break up. If you feel like crying your lungs out, breaking glasses, hitting the walls with your fists, screaming like hell just went loose- do so. It is part of your healing process. After all, we all have different methods of healing; some are just not as severe as others. Just do what you feel is right for you to get rid of the pain.

Your consistency of hiding your pain will lead to post traumatic stress disorder, depression and other worse cases.

In my case; I cried a lot to get over my partner. I sometimes got headaches, wallowed in self-pity and regret but it was part of my healing process. The thing you must also be aware of is the amount of time you have spent with your partner. You cannot compare a two year old relationship to a four month old relationship...These days, you are even lucky if your relationship makes it to a month! Of course, it is expected that the longer period relationship will be harder and more painful to get over. On the other hand, a short duration relationship might take a week and then the person will be okay.

I feel as adults, we step into relationships because we actually want to embark on life's journey with our partners...This means that even when you set your goals, you set them in such a way that they are able to accommodate your partner. Your entire life's schedule automatically starts to revolve around you and your partner. You plan things together...your careers, buying a house and starting a family for example.

So you can imagine the amount of trauma a break up can bring to your life when your "ideal" picture of life gets disrupted?!

So ladies; crying does not make you weak, instead it forms part of your recovery. Do me a favour; just know why you are crying. Most women cry, cry, cry and cry repetitively, over a failed relationship than to actually cry to get over their relationship. Do not just cry over your past; cry to get over your past.

Step 7: Ask for social support

Most people want to stay in their rooms and dwell in their sorrow on their own. Why? It makes no sense to me. You are risking your health and mental functioning.

Now there is something nice about asking your family for support; they will never judge you, especially your parents. In my case, my parents advised me not to date the person that I was dating. At that time, I just told myself they were crazy and that they did not want me to be happy.

I dated that person after being warned by my parents and brother. When things started to turn sour… Well, I did not want to tell my parents knowing very well that they would say that they warned me… Which indeed they did. So I was hard headed even to my parents' advice. See, I never thought that by telling me to leave my boyfriend, they were actually protecting me.

I used to be one of those people that would want to lock themselves in their rooms. I did not want to seek for help. I later learnt that the more I kept this pain hidden to myself, the more it broke me. At some point, I just had to swallow my pride and tell my mother about the whole break up. I also apologized for not listening to her advice. Instead of judging me, she supported and comforted me.

And because I shared my problems with someone, I started to feel better and started to even laugh more and more. It was at that very moment when I realised that it is not all the time that you will have to seek for professional support (like talking to a psychologist). Sometimes, you should just share your load with someone. I know that most people are not open to their parents about their problems. If you happen to be one of those people, I suggest you tell a friend or someone you can trust.

Once you do so, you will realize that it is actually stupid and unnecessary to stay alone in your room sucking your thumb.

Step 8: Forgive

Forgiveness is very important. Asking for forgiveness does not make you weak, instead it makes you strong. You also need to be able to forgive others, even if they did not ask for your forgiveness.

In one of his movies, Tyler Perry once mentioned how forgiveness is never about the other person but is for you. Carrying all the anger and bitterness is not good for you. You should therefore not allow yourself to suffer and become consumed by pain because of someone else's mistakes.

You may be hurt by a partner, but you need to wake up, get up, make peace and move on with your life. If you do not get up you are going to keep falling while your former partner is living. The fact remains that if you do not forgive that person, you are going to be stuck in your past, trying to raise the dead and that is not good for you. The truth is that not many ex partners feel guilty for breaking a woman's heart but that does not mean we should not forgive them.

You are worth a lot. Forgive that person and thank him for the role he has played in your life. Wish him well. Bless him. The sad part is that whether you forgive him or not, he is going to continue with his life, being happy and doing what pleases him. What about you? Are you going to dwell in sadness? Are you going to seek for revenge? My advice to you is simple… Forgive that person and start a new chapter in your life.

What is important for us to understand is what it actually means to apologise and to forgive as they are two different words that are used to ultimately restore peace. When one apologises, it actually means that they have acknowledged their wrong and they are regretful about it. In other words, the person who asks for an apology is the offender.

It is quite unfortunate that most of the time, the offender does not always acknowledge his or her offence.

If you are a victim and your offender does not acknowledge his or her wrong, it can put you in a bad space. As a victim, you will often feel like a fool, a nonentity, worthless, used, abused…the list goes on.

It often hurts more when the offence is committed by a person you actually trusted and relied on. The actual reason for that feeling is that you thought that person knows you and has your best interests at heart.

In the end, it does not really matter whether a person acknowledges that they have offended you or not. In reality, it does not change the fact that they have offended you. Whether a person apologises or not, does not change the fact that he or she has actually betrayed you. The acknowledgement of an offence may make you feel better but the crack of betrayal will still be there.

The nice thing about forgiveness is that it gives the victim power to take control of the situation. When you have been wronged, you are bound to feel guilty for actually trusting and relying on the person that offended you. The human brain somehow makes it so easy for us to actually blame ourselves for the betrayals of others. However, the only way you can escape that "self-guilt prison" is only through forgiving yourself. Forgive yourself for whatever you feel you may have done that could have led to you being offended.

Do not deprive yourself your actual right to happiness and mental freedom by bearing grudges. If you do not forgive yourself, you are going to remain stuck in the past, so just forgive yourself and move on. After forgiving yourself, you need to forgive your offender. For one, it could happen that your offender is not aware of his or her offence. It could also be that he or she is aware of it and does not care about the impact of his or her wrong doing on your emotional wellbeing.

Moreover, people sometimes just apologise for the sake of apologising because they know that it is what we want to hear from them. Hence you need to forgive the person that has wronged you and also decrease that person's room in your life thereafter.

Life is a precious gift that has been bestowed upon us. Hence we owe it to ourselves to be happy. Everything that we need to survive in life has been given to us including forgiveness.

Quoting from the Bible *"Love is patient, love is kind. It does not envy, it does not boast, it is not proud. It is not rude, it is not self-seeking, it is not easily angered, it keeps no record of wrongs. Love does not delight with evil but rejoices with the truth. It always protects, always trusts, always perseveres. Love never fails. And now these three remain: faith, hope and love. But the greatest of these is love*". We all need love, not only because we need to be loved but most importantly because God is love.

The fascinating fact about love is that it knows neither age nor boundaries. No drug can compare to love…Not even Whoonga! Hey! Be careful of that feeling.

Starting Afresh

When you decide to get into a relationship, do so for the right reasons. When you get into a relationship because you want to get over a break up or you are trying to feel whole… Then you are in a relationship for the wrong reasons. When you have such problems, you go to a psychologist not into another relationship! Getting into another relationship when your wound is still fresh is not a wise decision to make. Rather stay alone and find yourself and what you are going to do differently in your next relationship.

Bearing this in mind; there are times in life when you will feel like you have your whole life figured out. There are times when you will think that you have made enough back-ups in case of any mishaps. You will often feel certain that you do not want certain things in your life.

However, there will also come a time when you will become confronted by a challenging situation that you never thought could come your way. These challenges often disrupt our mind-sets…It could be your business failing, losing a loved one or even failing an exam. When that time comes, I advise you to just embrace that challenge and enjoy being in it. You should feel proud of being faced with that challenge. Furthermore, you must thank God for being confronted by that challenge because it is often the things that we fear that often reveal our strength.

The worst thing you can do to yourself, is settling with a man or woman that you "thought" you wanted because during your "very rushed" honeymoon phase, you felt like this woman or man was irreplaceable.

Then later, out of nowhere, things between you two just become complicated.

I am sure that you can agree with me that you have had at least one similar experience. These cases of "mistaken soulmates" and "false love" are very common. Some people choose to carry such pasts in their mind, whether it is intentional or unintentional is still questionable. Often, such memories (mistaken memories if you ask me) disturb the new relationship. These memories usually happen if and when, you have not dealt with your skeletons… your exes…your past.

At the top of your head; do you think your relationship is going to last whilst you are holding onto the carcasses of your previous relationship(s)? Is your relationship going to be strong enough to survive minor glitches?

One thing that I have learnt in life is that if you cannot accept what you cannot change, you are going to keep raising the dead.

Of course, you can attempt raising the dead. However, while attempting that, you must just remember that the dead and the living do not have anything in common. In other words, if you keep trying to make your present partner behave like your former partner, your relationship will be doomed. If you keep dwelling in your past, your present and future's progress will be hindered.

This is simple... If you meddle with your previous mistakes; your present situation will turn out exactly like your past mistakes because you will be placing too much focus on your past. Focusing on the things you have already failed on, will affect your current goals.

You will most likely fail again because you will still be stuck on your past. I have learned not to dwell on my mistakes and I want you to learn that too. I know it sounds easier said than done, but it will do you a lot of good to just bury that hatchet of your past mistakes!

Many times, I would do things thinking that I was doing them for myself…It later turned out that I was actually doings things for others because that was what they expected from me. These are things like getting good marks in high school, being a top performer in class, being in the school choir and being a leader in high school. These are good things but they were more externally influenced. It turns out that I was actually doing those things so that my parents could be proud of me and so that I do not shame the family.

During my first year in tertiary, academically I was still very strong but…I found myself surrounded by the wrong circle of friends.

By wrong circle of friends, I do not mean that they are purely bad influence; they were just not the right people for me. I just did not fit in. Then came 2015, my second year in tertiary and I still lived the same messed up life. That was just not me. That was not what I had envisioned for my life.

When 2016 came, I started to feel different about myself. Finally, I got to relax a bit and I started to find myself. I decided not to put too much pressure on myself and actually did things at my own pace. It is amazing how I changed in a matter of months. I got to view life differently and focused on me.

Growing up, I told myself "You know what Grace; you will never find a good partner. It is not that you have been cursed or something like that but it is because love is not meant for people like you".

It turned out that I did not find a person that loved me because I did not completely love myself…I always needed external validation.

The sad thing about external validation is that even if what you did was good; because someone is not commenting "positively" about it, you end up losing confidence in that thing. You also end up losing confidence in yourself. Breaking the chains of external validation is not easy. Setting oneself free from seeking approval from others demands that you sit down and tap into your sanity. You will have to sit down and figure out "why" you feel the need for others' approval.

That is when I discovered that the golden rule of love is to first love yourself completely so that you can be able to love others and that others can love you back… And whether you like it or not, you can see when a person has self-love.

So I went ahead and searched for the real me and fell in love with the real me. Right now I have love in my life and I am content. When you love yourself wholeheartedly, you complete yourself by default.

I actually feel like all the twenty years of my life I was just alive, but I only started living in 2016. It was only in 2016 that I did things that I like… Things that I always wanted to do…Things that actually define who I am. This has nothing to do with being twenty-one years old and having freedom. It is about me finding my purpose.

One thing that I have learnt is that unless you find your purpose and self-identity you will never be content with yourself.

Back then, I was always afraid of falling pregnant because of the life I lived. I thought that maybe I would not be a good mother and that I would punish an innocent child. However, when the pregnancy test results came back positive I was so happy. I started becoming responsible, eating right and focusing on the things that were important. It was a huge transition for me to move from a life of going out and partying to being a woman that ensures that there is food on the table, the house is clean and that my pregnancy was healthy. I feel like that is just who I am- a nurturer. I knew there and then that I had experienced growth and that I had become mature.

I also remember another defining moment that took place in my life. This happened during the year 2016 in varsity. I was going through my psychology text book and I just got stunned by the content of that book. I knew immediately just by browsing through that textbook that it was going to be a challenge to get good grades in psychology. This is because the module focused mainly on statistics and I resent numbers... Unless I have to count money of course.

I am passionate about psychology but I made up my mind there and then that although I know I love psychology, that time around I was not going to do so well in it. I just told myself that there are other modules I am good at and I will place my focus on them instead. I closed that chapter.

By making reference to that incident, I would like to urge you to stop stacking pain, mistakes and all the hurt of your past. All they do is consume your soul. I cannot emphasize the importance of letting go enough.

I cannot stress the importance of forgiving and moving on enough. Learn to let things go. However, when I say let go, I do not mean forget because once you forget, you are most likely to going to repeat the same mistake again. I know the Bible says that we should forgive and forget but according to what I have seen, forgetting is dangerous. If you forget you will have no record or reference of how similar incidents took place and how they ended up.

Take it like this- if you have failed a test and you do not find out how you got such low marks you are bound to fail again during an exam next time around…That is if you will even gain admission to write that exam.

I am one person that talks too much but most of the time I just tell the truth…My truth, rather. That is what is important- being able to tell the truth.

Over the years, I have grown and developed, hence I can fully admit that some of the decisions I made were as a result of me being rather very naïve. Most importantly, I was growing during that period of my life. However, a person does not stop growing. In order to be prosperous and live in peace, you cannot jump over certain stages of life. You have to go through all of those stages.

Most of these stages that we have to pass through, hurt us but it is life…Just please make sure you learn at least something from them.

Back then, I dated a lot of people…Hey I date! However, amongst all of those people I may have dated; I realized that I was not in a relationship with most them. They did not even add much value to my life. At that time, I would become angry and bitter and I felt like "I do not want to talk to this person ever again" once what we had was over. Of course people will tell you that you will get better in time but I did not care about what they had to say, I was just mad.

However, today, as I sit down and reflect, I actually thank God for allowing those people into my life. If not for them, I would not have known which people are right for me. If not for them I would also not have become the woman that I am today. I actually needed that mental challenge and experience in order to grow.

So, I would really like to thank those people for treating me the way they did because they made me a better person. I do not know about you but my former partners taught me how to cook, clean, respect and take care of my partner. Hence I will forever be grateful for them for preparing me for my life partner…Who I am still waiting for by the way.

As a person, it is advisable that you see beyond your pain. Do not look at your pain as a setback; rather look at it as preparation for the joy you are going to feel and experience in future.

Your life can be the way that you want it to be. Whatever you do, be it drinking every day, hooking up with every man, I do not care. Your actions should just be as a result of your own personal choice and decision.

This is because at the end of the day, you do not want to sit down and blame someone else for the way your life has turned out. It does not matter if you were young or foolish because at the end of the day you are the one that personally agreed on doing that particular thing.

I, for one, have accepted that even though the people that I thought cared about me actually used me- it is okay. We live in a dog eat dog world, where the fittest survive and the weak and meek are not taken into consideration. So I cannot blame people for what I went through, simply because I had a weakness and they were able to spot it and actually took advantage of it.

I learnt that when it comes to life, you should never tell yourself that you have got it all figured out. We live in a world of uncertainties. We all know that life is unpredictable.

The weather forecasters can tell us that tomorrow it is going to be sunny then it ends up raining. Such is life. However, the fact that life is unpredictable; does not mean we should not plan for our lives.

Imagine having to wake up every morning without having any plan or goal to achieve... That would be disastrous. That attitude is the reason why people fail in life. People who fail to plan ahead fail because for one, they accept whatever life throws at them without giving it a challenge. Most of the time these same people will often say "I am tired" or "I cannot do this". Question is; what did you want to achieve for that day, month or year?

No one is 100% decisive regarding what he or she wants to achieve but you should at least have an idea of what you want to achieve. Often, we alter our goals as we proceed with them.

However, as a person you should know that if something turns out negatively in your life, it will be as a result of your mistakes, actions and your willingness for that negativity to occur in your life. I once met this gentleman. He said to me that he met the wrong women almost all his life and that now he is afraid of being with a decent woman because he does not know which woman is decent. He went even further to say that "People assume that I am still a player because of the things that I did in my past. I dated a lot of girls and though I knew some of them were good, I still discarded them like they meant nothing". You know what I liked about what he had to say? I liked the fact that he kept on saying "I" did this and that.

This clearly shows that whatever you do always points back to you. It does not matter how many times you sit with a group of friends… Whenever you do something wrong or right, it will always be a reflection of you and who you are. It does not matter if you were given a "mandate" by your group leader, when something goes wrong, it will point right back at you as the executor of that particular act.

As people we are also rotten in perfection. It is automatically inherent in us that we can achieve so much more. This explains why we end up getting hurt when we cannot achieve that "more" that we want. We therefore need to learn to limit our room for perfection.

Your friend or significant other may be good in physics and you in computers. However, instead of you focusing on your strength which in this case is computers, you may want to focus on physics because you think that if your friend is good in it, you can also be good in it. This happens quite a lot! We tend to become so lost in life because we think that we need to do that which the world thinks is better instead of focusing on our qualities. I do not know why we even try so hard to do things that were not meant for us. As a person you need to know what is not meant for you.

You will keep on failing at something because that particular thing you are focusing on is not meant for you. It is time for you to start searching for what you are good at. Once you find that strength of yours, focus on it.

Get this. People usually say to fail is "First Attempt In Learning". Now, what happens if you fail again? Then it is no longer FAIL instead it is SAIL (Second Attempt In Learning) meaning that you are going down. If you fail once more, it is no longer SAIL. It then becomes TAIL, meaning you are going below the survival chain. Always remember that the lower you sink, the harder it becomes for you to get up. The moment you realise that the more you try, you fail, you need to stop and think on what you could be doing wrong. You can only try so much before you become demotivated.

As a person you need to be responsible for your actions and account to them. Stop pointing fingers but also be careful who you let into your life. You should not inhibit who you are just so another person can feel accommodated in your life. If people want to feel and be accommodated in your life, they should get in your life and accept you with your baggage. It is only fair because you also have to accept them with the baggage that they come with into your life.

Most of time when we step into relationships, a lot of things ponder in our minds..."Do I need this person? Will this person be there for me?". When all is said and done, all that you should pray for, is that God introduces you to "the one". The one does not have to be the one that marries you. Instead he or she should be that companion that will sail through life with you...

That person should be the one to teach you in life and help you grow... This is not because they know it all but because we cannot sail through life alone.

Stop formulating checklists for the perfect man or following articles from magazines that contain "the 10 signs that show he or she is the one". Stop asking your friends whether they have seen your possible life partner in clubs, drinking with girls etcetera. Hey! The fact that people go to clubs does not mean that they are scouting for a pound of flesh for the night…People have stress! They go to clubs because they want to offload life's stress. Do not get this misconception that people are alcoholics or "busy" just because they go out.

Asking yourself whether he or she is the right one will not get you anywhere. If you want to know whether you are looking at the right person, do yourself a favour and go down on your knees. Ask God to show you signs whether that person is right for you! Believe me God will show you the signs that you are looking for. Most of the time we choose to take these signs for granted.

You must always bear in mind that who you want and who God wants for you are two different things. Allow God to take the driver's seat in your life.

Let Him be the one who dictates who should become a part of your life. And just because a person was brought into your life by God does not mean that he or she should not leave you! If a person's chapter in your life is over, he or she will go and you will have to turn the page.

If you are now going to carry all the pain once a person leaves you…Going around hurting other people just because you chose to carry the pain of someone that left you…You are only breaking yourself!

Stop holding onto pain of the past. Stop wondering about what could have been. Stop saying you cannot find someone you can love because it is not the right time yet.

Stop saying your life is too messed up for you to accommodate someone else in it. The right person will welcome you and your mess with open arms!

You deserve to be happy. You deserve to be with someone who makes you happy. You deserve to be with someone who values you. You deserve to be with someone who sees your purpose in life…sometimes without you even realizing it.

Do not be involved with someone who puts you down… Be with someone who can pick you up when you are at your weakest!

References

Holy Bible, New International Version, 2011. Biblica Inc, https://www.biblegateway.com/passage/?search=1+Corinthians+13&version=NIV [Accessed on 12 October 2018]

Jackson, M N/A. *Speechless lyrics*, Sony/ATV Music Publishing LLC, Warner/Chappell Music Inc, https://www.google.co.za/search?q=speechless+lyrics&rlz=1C1GCEB_enZA824ZA824&oq=speecghless&aqs=chrome.3.69i57j0l5.7255j0j4&sourceid=chrome&ie=UTF-8 [Accessed 12 October]

Vandross, L N/A. *I'd rather lyrics*, Universal Music Publishing Group, https://www.google.co.za/search?q=id+rather+kyrics&rl

z=1C1GCEB_enZA824ZA824&oq=id+rather+kyrics&aqs=chrome..69i57j0l5.7071j0j4&sourceid=chrome&ie=UTF-8[Accessed on 12 October 2018]